The Pink Corner Office

The Pink
Corner Office

Women Achieving Power
In The Workplace

Suzanne Y. Penn, Ph.D.

Copyright © 2006 by Suzanne Y. Penn, Ph.D..

Library of Congress Control Number:		2006905088
ISBN 10:	Hardcover	1-4257-2117-6
	Softcover	1-4257-2116-8
ISBN 13:	Hardcover	978-1-4257-2117-6
	Softcover	978-1-4257-2116-9

All rights reserved. No part of this book may be reproduced or transmitted in any form or by any means, electronic or mechanical, including photocopying, recording, or by any information storage and retrieval system, without permission in writing from the copyright owner.

This book was printed in the United States of America.

To order additional copies of this book, contact:
Xlibris Corporation
1-888-795-4274
www.Xlibris.com
Orders@Xlibris.com

30370

Contents

PREFACE 7

CHAPTER I: OUR UNIQUE STRESSES 9

CHAPTER II: OUR OBSTASTCLES 15

CHAPTER III: OUR STRATEGIES FOR SUCCESS 27

CHAPTER IV: OUR FUTURE 49

CHAPTER V: OUR NEXT STEP 52

INDEX 69

REFERENCES 71

PREFACE

This is a book on women in management, executive and professional positions in the workplace. Since the 1970s women began moving into higher-level positions in the workplace in large numbers. Before the twentieth century women rarely gained leadership positions in companies. In fact, during the end of the nineteenth century the woman's role was traditionally and historically subservient to men. Our role as women was to work in the home, and be a wife and a mother. Still today, women face gender discrimination in the workplace. Women are not paid equally to men, and women are often perceived stereotypically as being inferior to men. There continues to be a glass ceiling within corporations. Women with high-level positions are also challenged with the pressure of balancing work and family responsibilities. Yet, women who are persistent and use wise strategies to succeed continually make significant accomplishments in the workplace to promote their careers and to bring success to their organizations. This book is about studying the issues that we as women face, quantifying our opinions, and providing solutions for where we need to go from here.

CHAPTER I

OUR UNIQUE STRESSES

Introduction

Since the 1970s, women have made remarkable strides for better paying positions in the workplace. In 1997, in the U.S., women were 2.5 percent of the top earners in Fortune 500 companies; women were 5.3 percent of corporate officers, and held 10.6 percent of board seats for Fortune 500 companies. Throughout the world, particularly in industrialized nations, women have moved up significantly in corporate organizations. In Canada, women hold 12 percent of the CEO seats for Financial Post 500 companies, which is equivalent to U.S. Fortune 500 companies (Women in Management, 1999). However, as women moved up the ladder of success in corporations, they soon learned that they would face obstacles to moving into senior management and higher-level executive positions.

Ellig and Morin (2001) explain that though women have gone a long way and many women hold management, executive and professional positions in corporations today, women are still faced with challenges at the top:

1. Of the Fortune 500 companies, only two women are at the leadership—Hewlett Packard and Avon.
2. In the high ranks of top companies in corporate America, 83 women and 2,267 men hold positions as chairman, CEO, COO, vice chairman, president, and senior and executive vice president.
3. As top earners in leadership, women hold 2.7 percent of the top earner positions, which is only 63 of 2,320 in top earning positions of Fortune 500 companies.

Ellig and Morin (2001) cite that women in management share a common complaint:

> The opportunities just aren't being offered; we aren't moving up fast enough, and we're deeply angered when we see less capable men getting the choicest positions and CEOs, with poor corporate performance records being handsomely rewarded, the meritocracy value becomes meaningless. Where is the investment in us? (Ellig and Morin, 2001, p. 3-4)

A 1999 report for the Society of Human Resource Management cites five barriers to advancement for women in corporate America:

1. A culture that favors men;
2. Men's stereotypical preconceptions of women;
3. Lack of female representation on corporate boards;
4. Women's exclusion from informal networks and;
5. Management perceptions read that women will be hampered by family responsibilities.

(Ellig and Morin, 2001, p. 4)

Women control 80 percent of $3 trillion consumer spending in the U.S., yet still companies do not focus their marketing on women (Ellig and Morin, 2001).

Montana (1996) states that it may appear that professional women have it made with a privileged life, and that they are protected from gender biases those working class women with non-management positions may face. Professional women have high salaries, rewarding jobs, more flexibility and personal independence, and appear to have overcome the pitfalls that women typically face relative to work. However, this picture is not completely true. Women with professional positions face more gender bias than women with non-management positions. This is because professional women encounter men in more challenging settings that threaten male dominance as they attain higher education and strive to succeed in organizations professionally. Professional women face potential discrimination and exploitation in sometimes-unique ways as they encounter more roadblocks on their high attaining path of life (Montana, 1996).

This book identifies, describes, and analyzes the issues and challenges that a woman in the workplace faces.

Background

The increased number of women in the workforce with better paying jobs was the result of five major changes in U.S. economy and society:

1. Technological advances, which launched the demand for more typists, stenographers and file clerks.
2. Population growth.
3. Expansion of urban areas due to population growth, new businesses, and the demand for more construction of new homes.
4. Economic growth, which caused more jobs to be created that required more workers.
5. Women gained more rights due to feminist organizations that changed the legal and political system giving women equal rights.

(Smith, 2000)

Traditional Roles for Women

In the past, our traditional role as women was identified as a helpmate to men:

> . . . And the Lord God said, it is not good that man should be alone; I will make a helper for him . . . and the Lord God caused a deep sleep to fall upon Adam . . . and he took one of his ribs, and closed up the flesh . . . thereof . . . and the rib, which the Lord God had taken from man, made he a woman, and brought her unto the man . . . and Adam said, this is now bone of my bones, and flesh of my flesh: and she shall be called Woman, because she was taken out of man. (Life Application Bible, 1989, p. 1)

Before the mid-twentieth century, women were looked upon as the weaker sex. There was the belief that women could not perform tasks requiring muscular or intellectual capabilities. When, in fact, most of the domestic chores that women performed at home required much muscular ability, such as milking cows and washing clothes; and when educated, women excel as well as men. But because women gave birth to children, their role was viewed through maternity with the stereotypical role of a woman's place being in the home (Blackwell, 1989). Some men hold the belief that women can never rise above a man. However, this untrue concept is due to the fact that many men in the past had become used to asserting power over women (Clark, 1983).

Unfortunately, in the past, some women themselves bought into the concept that their place was in the home, seeing themselves as inferior to men, and satisfied with serving men according to an unequal status. Even today, as women have been freed from the bounds of stereotypical roles of inferiority, some talented women, who have achieved higher education, high-level jobs, and leadership roles in many fields, are still plagued with societal pressures to become wives and mothers. As a result, many successful career women opt to quit their jobs and abandon their careers to become full-time wives and mothers (Clark, 1983).

Balancing work and family has caused many women to face more obstacles and pressures than men. Men throughout history have had no restraints on the type of work they take or the hours they worked, while women were seen primarily as caretakers and all other pursuits were considered secondary to child care (Clark, 1983). The woman's role historically has also been relegated to caring for elderly parents, and women's careers are often interrupted due to their roles as caretakers to their children and elderly parents (Atkinson and Fredrick, 1997).

The traditional corporate model of success for men was to be married to a woman who is a housewife. The wife's role was to support her husband's career and interests. For some African American families, women have historically worked, but not in higher-level positions, to help support the family income. In the last thirty years, inferiority concepts regarding women have changed as women began fulfilling their desires to have successful careers in meaningful positions while also taking care of the home and family, with men increasingly assisting with tasks to run the home and rear the children (Atkinson and Fredrick, 1997)

Women Move into Professional Careers in the 20th Century

Women are no longer mostly homemakers, but have moved into the workforce remarkably. Today many women are directors, vice presidents, and leaders within organizations. Women comprise 40 percent of the workforce today (www.uwvo.edu, 2005). In 1960, only 30 percent of young women in college believed that they would be working at age thirty. This is partly because at that time women were not admitted to prestigious universities for undergraduate programs. Women were not customarily admitted to Harvard until 1963, Yale until 1969, and Columbia until 1983.

Before women were accepted at the best universities they mostly attended women's colleges, some of which were very good schools, but these were not the top universities (Gallagher, 2000).

Times have changed. In 2000, women were earning 35 percent of MBA degrees up from 3.6 percent in 1970, and 42 percent of law degrees up from 5.4 percent. Today many women earn a large number of degrees at the Ivy League colleges. And 48.9 percent of those working as managers and professionals are women. Yet, women still face many obstacles to advance in their careers (Gallagher, 2000).

Unique Stresses

According to Gearing (2000), on a daily basis, women battle for legitimacy in the workplace. They must endure criticisms that all women bear in the workplace, and struggle with biases about women in power. Women in leadership roles are still considered unfeminine by men and women. In the study by Gearing (2000), it was cited that 87 percent of women executives from throughout the country face unique stresses. Women experience unique pressures in the workplace, which Gearing (2000) calls the Female Executive Stress Syndrome:

1. They feel that they have to give 150 percent to hold their own with male counterparts.
2. They earn less income than male peers in the same position.
3. They are cut off from the "good old boys" network in informal settings, i.e. the golf course, men's lounges in country clubs, and other after work activities that men traditionally share.
4. Other women in the workplace, who hold the same kinds of negative views as men about women in power, undermine them.
5. They must deal with sexual harassment and sexism, which includes lewd comments, touching, and inappropriate kisses.
6. They often have no role models or support system of peers, which make it lonely at the top for senior female management.

(Gearing, 2000)

Women executives state that balancing the stresses of work and then encountering challenges when they get home, with limited time for family, is like having to live with two personalities. Additionally, in their personal lives they have few friends because being a top executive; they now have a different lifestyle than old friends. Traveling for their job limits their contact with personal friends. Senior women professionals are often left feeling guilty about how their work interferes with their family role. Unless the culture changes, many professional women will continually be subjected to stresses that could lead to the Female Executive Stress Syndrome (Gearing, 2000). Many women have become dissatisfied with inequity and stresses in their jobs, and as a result have gone into business (Small Business, 2002). Sales for women owned businesses increased 33 percent from 1992 to 1997, versus an increase of 24 percent for all non-publicly owned companies for that period (Small Business, 2002).

CHAPTER II

OUR OBSTASTCLES

This book examines the dilemmas that women face in the workplace and identifies strategies that women have taken to succeed and become empowered in the workplace. This book analyzes the phenomena of women in the workplace, and the opportunities, achievements as well as barriers that women experience in higher-level positions. This study can be fundamental to pointing out the qualities and actions that bring success to women in the workplace. Due to the collection of relevant data regarding women in the workplace that this study presents in detail, it is an important instrument that can be essential to addressing the issues that women face and how they can be successful in higher-level positions.

In a study by Swiss (1996), it was explained that 325 diverse women in a cross section of organizations revealed that there was a gap in opportunities and policies for men and women on the job, which significantly impacts women's careers and lives. The Swiss (1996) study included women participants in senior, middle and lower management, in the fields of "finance, law, telecommunication, banking, insurance, consulting, marketing, real estate, general management, manufacturing, medicine, engineering and science" (Swiss, 1996, p. 2). The size of the companies was small to large; yet, most women in the study agree that gender bias is persistent in their company. Regarding pace of advancement, standards of performance, compensation, opportunities to take risk professionally, access to build business relationships, and support received from top management, there is differential and exclusionary treatment relative to gender, even for stellar performing women managers. However, women are beginning to address these issues by taking actions and applying strategies to bring down obstacles that are barriers to women in the workplace (Swiss, 1996).

For minority women, black, Asian and Hispanic, they hold 5.6 percent of management jobs, and are underrepresented compared to white women. Sixty percent of women of color that are managers tend to cluster in some of the lowest paying industries, i.e. retail trade, professional-related services, finance, insurance, and real estate (Catalyst, 2000).

Today, women in the workplace still face many challenges and much gender discrimination. Women encounter gender challenges in which they have to conform to male norms and games, women are still not paid equally as men, women are often stereotyped as being inferior to men, and there is the glass ceiling that inhibits a woman's promotion to the highest levels of management and executive positions. Additionally, professional women are challenged with the balancing act of coordinating work and family responsibilities, sexual harassment, and organizational management that is apprehensive about women having leadership positions challenges women.

Gender Discrimination

Gender discrimination is done in various forms and disguises, and cannot easily be identified. In fact, sometimes gender discrimination is so subtle that a woman may not realize it has occurred. According to Women in Wireless Communication (2005), in the Information Technology (IT) industry, women were directly told that it was a man's field, and women were discouraged from entering or staying in the field until recently.

Gender roles are the influence of biological, societal and environmental factors. Gender roles influence how their parents, teachers, peers, and everyone in their life treat individuals as boys and girls growing up; and unfortunately define their success in careers as adults (Smith, 2000). Women face constant challenges as they strive to climb the corporate ladder. There is a double standard in the workplace, whereas women have to work twice as hard as men to receive moderate recognition though she is equal and often more qualified than men. When men perform a task well, he often receives a bonus, while women seldom receive a bonus for a job well done. The double standard is even more prevalent when it involves a woman of color (Smith, 2000). For promotions, managers, who still assume that a woman's role will sooner or later become focused on mothering rather than her career, often overlook women. Many males in organizations hold a concept of women that looks at the possibility of a woman one day bearing children instead of her qualifications and capabilities at work (Smith, 2000).

Playing the Man's Game to Succeed

In the past, women were faced with the dilemma of being feminine while commanding a dominate position on the job, and to move up within an organization they had to play the male's game by the male's rules (Glaser and Smalley, 1995). As women have entered professional positions in large numbers, they face many challenges in what is still primarily a male-dominated society and workplace. It is perceived that a woman cannot become an authority figure because she is not "one of the boys," unless she can act like a man and play by men's rules (Fredrick and Atkinson, 1997). Glaser and Smalley (1995) explain that as women began moving into higher level management and executive positions in large numbers in the 1970s, they were finding themselves having to "fit in" and making themselves over "from caring to tough, motivating to controlling, and empowering to overpowering" (p. 2). They had to swim with the sharks, when they were not sharks, but more like dolphins.

However, as the 1990s arrived, women were reaching for success under their own terms, which has changed corporate America. This change was provoked by a changing economy. America went from it's industrial age to the information age with the global economy, which requires motivating the workforce, something at which women excel. Today women are increasingly playing the corporate game by their own rules, as individuals, and not as individuals packaged as a male within a female body (Glaser and Smalley, 1995).

The days of the "old boys club" are gone. Higher management is becoming leaders, coaches, facilitators, mentors, and friends to their subordinates. Today, there is more of a dolphin approach to business to attract, hire and keep good employees. The focus is on building effective teams, sharing tasks, motivating staff, having win-win relationships with employees, and women are highly effective in these focuses (Glaser and Smalley, 1995).

Women's Salaries are Less than Men's

Gender discrimination affects both a woman's employment experience and her paycheck (www.albany.edu). Just as unequal salaries was a problem for working women in the 1920s, this problem still exist today. According to the Bureau of Labor Statistics, in 1979, women's salaries were only 59.7 percent of men. According to the Department of Labor, in a 1992 report, women that work full-time, year around receive 72.2 percent of men in the same field and doing the same work. "When we talk of comparing women's earnings with men's earnings, we find that no matter how we measure them, women's earnings are below those received by men" (www.dol.gov, 2005, p. 1). This gap has closed little to date across gender, race, age, and ethnic groups:

> For those who are 25-54 years old, the most striking trend has been the high earnings of white men compared with all other race, ethnic, and gender groups. For those 55 or older . . . White men's earnings are substantially above all other groups. (www. dol.gov, 2005, p. 4)

According to the U.S. Department of Labor (2000), the salary gap of men and women closed only 20 percent from 1979 to 1999. Though the salary gap has narrowed, it took twenty years to do so (Bulletin to Management, 2001). The weekly earnings gap of women in 1997 was 23.5 percent less than men, and the annual gap earnings was 27.8 percent below men. The income of women in 1999 by hourly pay was 16.2 percent less than men (Catalyst, 2000). It must be noted that women work fewer hours each week and fewer weeks per year than men, which results in a small amount for the discrepancy of pay; yet, it must also be noted that overall women's pay is below men for the same work.

Gender Stereotyping

Even though women have made significant strides and are becoming recognized as valuable assets in upper management, professional and executive positions, there still exists considerable gender stereotyping. According to Atkinson and Fredrick (1997), there are a number of factors that men cite that appears based on stereotypical perceptions and prevent women from obtaining senior positions in the workplace, which include: women are not knowledgeable of corporate politics, women are not effective leaders, women do not have what it takes to take on leadership positions, and the woman's role is family responsibilities. Some CEOs cite that women lack experience and have not been in the "pipeline" long enough to advance to leadership roles.

Even today, some theorists argue the Darwin law as a reason for many women remaining in lower salary, lower status positions. In 1998, Kingsley Browne, a well-known evolution theorists, claimed that women are not genetically designed to succeed in the workplace, and will always hold lower paying jobs with lower status due to their lack of competitiveness:

> Men have more commitment to the labor market than women, who place more importance on their children. Given an economic system that rewards competition and high levels of workplace investment, women are unlikely to achieve parity with men, even if discrimination against women is completely eradicated. (People Management, 1998, p. 21)

Browne also states that traditional indicators of success in management, such as risk taking and focusing on tasks and skills, are behavior traits mainly found in men (People Management, 1998).

Allan Pease, a training consultant and author, contends that the skill levels of men and women are different because of the difference in "brain wiring." Pease claims that women have poor spatial awareness, which is a reason why nearly all air traffic controllers, are men. He states that people intuitively know that sexual sameness is wrong (People Management).

Caudron (1994) cited a study in which 79 percent of CEOs agreed that there is stereotyping by gender in the workplace that impedes women's career advancement:

> Prejudice and stereotypes are among the most identifiable barriers to women's advancement in U.S. corporations. The stereotypes reported with the highest frequency were that women lack career commitment, are not tough enough, don't want to work long or unusual hours, are too emotional, won't relocate, lack quantitative and analytical skills and have trouble making decisions. (Caudron, 1994, p. 31)

However, Markson (1996) explains that though there are genetic traits within humans, skills of men and women are not exclusive. People have natural aptitudes; they have the ability to learn. To state that women are destined to lower paying, lower status positions due to genetic programming is simplistic and out of step with this new millennium. Women are especially skilled at communication and teamwork relations:

Woman's management style, which centers on communication and positive working relationships, is better suited than men's to the team-oriented leadership of the 90's. (www.leadership-development.com, 2005, p. 1)

According to the Catalyst (2000), both women and men are prejudiced toward women in the workplace. In studies conducted with both men and women as respondents on evaluating work performance, findings were in favor of men performing more competently, which shows that there is lower perceived value of women in society overall. Findings show that it is perceived if women can do a task, it is not difficult (Catalyst, 1997). It must be noted that much of the perceptions about competence or incompetence relative to gender is influenced by the traditional roles of men and women.

The media plays a large role in presenting stereotypical images of males and females differently. The media is in our lives daily, and it is virtually impossible to escape the influence of television, movies, newspapers, magazine, music, video games, and advertisements. Often in the media, women's physical attractiveness and sexuality is the focus as much as allowed by the law, which is the Federal Communication Commission (FCC). Frequently women's cleavage and legs in short shirts are shown, and increasingly girls are showing their bellies and wear even shorter skirts in the media, while dynamic roles that require intellectual interactions are rarely given to female actresses (Smith, 2000).

The Glass Ceiling

In the last twenty years, as women have started entering jobs that have been traditionally held by men, i.e. law, business, politics, education, and science, many people believe that getting to the top of these fields is a matter of hard work. However, the number of women that have made it to the top of their field is still small, and the glass ceiling though invisible is still in place. The glass ceiling is virtually invisible until someone crashes into it (Swoboda, 1995).

The term glass ceiling refers to the level that women, particularly women in management and executives, could not be allowed to rise above. Perceptions of the glass ceiling are real, though the excuses that prevent women from penetrating the glass ceiling can vary from structural barriers, educational barriers, or experience barriers (Smith, 2000).

The 1995 Federal Glass Ceiling Commission cited that women are gaining few power positions in corporations in America, that women are 5 percent of senior managers, vice presidents and higher within Fortune 500 companies; and at the highest levels of companies there are barriers that are rarely penetrated by women or people of color (Kanter, 1997). The Commission cited that the nation's boardrooms remain overwhelmingly male. Ninety-five percent of senior-level management in Fortune 1000 industries and Fortune 500 corporations are men, and 97 percent are white (Swoboda, 1995) (See Table 1).

Table 1.Ratio of Women to Men in Administrative Positions

Country	Female/Male
Canada	68/100
United States	67/100
New Zealand	48/100
Cuba	23/100
Poland	18/100
Japan	9/100
India	2/100

(Swoboda, 1995)

Even for women that surpass the glass ceiling, they reach a point where there is a second glass ceiling that prevents them from reaching the highest executive positions. Men at the top have more perks and career opportunities than women in high level positions (See Table 2). When women earn the same pay and bonuses as male executives, they tend to manage fewer people, have fewer stock options, and gain fewer foreign assignments than male executives. Additionally, women tend to have less status and clout at top management than men, and women report more obstacles, less satisfaction, and less future career opportunities than men at the top. Despite excellent track records, it is believed by many high level executives that women will not do as well as male executives in their job (Women in Management, 1999).

Table 2.Glass Ceiling Perks are Different for Men and Women

Men	Women
Larger paycheck	Smaller paycheck
Larger bonuses	Sometimes no bonus at all
Larger staff to manage	Very few staff to manage
More stock options	Fewer stock options
Foreign assignments	Seldom offered foreign assignments
Offered new opportunities	Moved as far as they can with few new opportunities

(Women in Management, 1999)

Gallagher (2000) states that thirty percent of women opt out of the corporate world to become entrepreneurs or work part-time. For the other 70 percent, who remain and interact in the complex game of power in big business, they continually strive to break through the glass ceiling (Gallagher 2000).

Balancing Work and Family Responsibilities

A two-paycheck household has the benefits of higher income for the home. Additionally, dual career couples are reported as having more personal fulfillment, intellectual equality of the genders, and emotional support for each other. Higher quality day care centers and increased flexibility of hours at work make it possible for both spouses to work, and reduce the stress of balancing work and home. Unfortunately the responsibility for childcare and juggling job flexibility still tend to fall on the woman (West, 1995).

Holding down a demanding job and responsibilities at home can cause spillover for many women with professional careers. Work-to-family spillover refers to the impact that a job role has on family duties; and family-to-work spillover is how the demands at home impact demands at work (www.uwvo. edu, 2005). Yet, today, most women desire to be more than a homemaker and desire careers. As homemakers, women tend to place less focus on their education, and tend to let their certificates lapse by not keeping the certifications they have acquired up-to-date (Smith, 2000; Rosener, 1995). According to the U.S. Department of Labor, 57 million women work in the U.S., 70 percent work full time and 28 percent work part time; forty percent have children under age 18, and 16 percent have children under age 6 (Smith, 2000).

In a study by Stoner and Hartman (1990), 1500 female managers were interviewed to show the activities women have engaged in to deal with the dual responsibility of work and family. Thirty percent state that balancing home and career affect their career due to: maternity leave, altering career expectations, and limited career choices.

Maternity Leave

Though it is customary for women to take maternity leave from work, female managers believe that it can jeopardize their careers. Most women managers believe that maternity leave can hold up their career, interfere with them gaining promotions, cause loss of career momentum, and lose a professional woman's place in the mainstream of the organization. Most organizations look unfavorably upon female managers with children, despite the fact that 71 percent of mothers with children under age 18 are employed (Cannings and Montmarquette, 2000).

Altering Career Expectations

A large number of women with a career and children state that they have to split their time between career and family, and do not have adequate time needed to complete job expectations. Many women with children are not available before and after work for meetings, socializing with clientele, travel, and overtime. Thus, personally, many female managers with children may be less committed to their jobs as needed, which can harm their careers (Cannings and Montmarquette, 2000).

Career Choice

Many women stated that their career choice was based on location, flexible schedule, convenient hours, and other determinants such as childcare at the work site. As a result, many women put their career plans aside in favor of a career that is conducive to their family needs (Cannings and Montmarquette, 2000).

Significance Of This Book

In this book, pertinent information is provided on how women can challenge obstacles against women in the workplace, foster their careers, and excel within corporations to promote organizational success, and balance work and family responsibilities. This book can serve as an instrument that provides important information regarding how women in the workplace can be recognized and promoted in their work. The empowerment of women that creates successful management, executives, and professionals is examined in this study.

Qualities that promote characteristics of proficient leadership are the qualities that women must foster to succeed in the workplace. The relationship of women in the workplace with other higher-level personnel is a fundamental ingredient to bring success for women in the workplace (Smith, 2000). In a study conducted by Alfred (2005), it was found that for women to progress in the workplace and gain economic self-sufficiency, personal and structural barriers must be addressed. Women must implement effective strategies to achieve success in what is still considered "a man's world" by many men and women.

Leathwood (2005) states that women create their own gender identity within the workplace, and must work to construct new identities that foster empowerment relationships. Silver (2004) describes women in management as: "not only energetic but single minded in pursuit of her goal; she has a mission and clear vision; she intends to create out of this vision a product or service (Silver, 2004, p. 1).

In a natural corporate structure, due to complex corporate challenges to adapt to the uncertainty and constant evaluation of the global economy, women's traits are becoming valuable to the new global economy (Hirsh and Jackson, 1989). Women's management approach of relational consultation and democratic decision-making is increasingly more important to organizations (Grant, 1988). Drucker (1994) states that in the new information age, teamwork rather than individualism is more valuable for business success.

In a study by Kabacoff (1998), it was found that women have a higher rate of empathy to be concerned for the needs of others, women form close supportive relationships, they communicate by stating clearly their expectations and thoughts and ideas, and maintain a flow of communication more than men. Women have more people skills and hold high expectations for themselves and others, while men rate higher on strategic planning and organizational vision. Men are more hierarchical oriented, in which there is an importance for rank order to be clear to everyone present and a winner must be established. While women are more teamwork oriented (Kabacoff, 1998). Yet, Cava (1988) explains that women are "three times more likely to sacrifice their careers for the sake of marriage and child rearing" (p. 1). Being a woman can be precarious and a woman cannot count on a man's support all her life. Seventy-five percent of women never marry, are widows, divorced, or separated.

According to the U.S. Census Bureau, in 1970 the median income for men was $9,223, and $5,412 for women, in which women earned 59 cents for each dollar earned by men. In 2000, the median income for men was $38,870, and $28,080 for women, in which women earned 73 cents for each dollar earned by men. In the last thirty years, the gap in wages for men and women has narrowed only 14 cents, and at this rate it will take women another 66 years before the wage gap for women and men closes (Fredrick and Atkinson, 1997).

This book is beneficial to promoting women in the workplace as it extends significant knowledge to this subject. As American businesses face the challenge to succeed in this new millennium of global economy, effective management and executives are crucial regardless rather an individual wears a skirt. Women bring new work approaches to the workplace, which are beneficial to dynamic leadership.

Our Purpose

The purpose of this book on women in the workplace is to identify, examine and describe the issues and experiences of women working in professional positions. Strategies of women's success in the workplace as described in this study are instrumental to comprehending the phenomena of women in the workplace overall. The objective of this study is to examine and explain how women in the workplace can be empowered and effective in their roles to improve business practices in this new global economy. The focus of this study is on women in management, executive and professional positions in American companies, and also discuss women overall in the workplace in lower level positions, and in other nations.

This book also explains why women can also make great leaders. The intention of this study is to help you understand why so many women in the workforce struggle every day with the concept of always trying to prove to themselves and others, especially to men, that they are as good, if not better than the "rest" (Smith, 2000).

Questions To Ask Yourself

The goal is to illustrate how the structure of a corporation impacts women in the workplace. We must ask ourselves these four questions:

1. Are their opportunities for professional advancement for women in the workplace?
2. Are women treated and promoted differently than men in the workplace?
3. Do societal traditions and gender stereotyping interfere with opportunities for women to achieve in the workplace?
4. Do women face challenges balancing their roles at work and their family responsibilities?

CHAPTER III

OUR STRATEGIES FOR SUCCESS

Barriers to Women in the Workplace

While women tend to be ambitious, even more than men in many cases, women still face a dilemma when faced with being assertive and power-seeking, which are characteristic of leaders. Assertiveness and power seeking while attractive in men are seen as hostility and aggression in a woman (Kanter, 1997). Kanter (1997) identified the barriers that keep women from accessing top level positions:

1. Women do not exercise their roles and behaviors in authoritarian ways.
2. Women are unaggressive, and avoid conflicts.
3. Women are too accessible; their doors are always open.
4. Women are personality oriented, relationships are important to them.
5. Women seek approval, and are indirect, which can be identified in their speech.
6. Women want to be nice, fear abuse of power, and are hesitant.
7. Women attribute their success to others.
8. Women feel that their abilities are unequal to men's abilities.
9. Women avoid the appearance of success, in attempts to be socially appropriate.
10. Women are socialized as children to not be aggressive and assertive, or to seek power and control.

11. Women tend to be more easily swayed and rely too much on others.

12. Women in top positions tend to internalize, and are too sensitive. (Kanter, 1997)

In the past, how some women managers overcame these dilemmas was to behave entirely like their male counterparts. However, today's hierarchical structure in organizations are focused on training, teamwork, sharing of power and information, and networking, which are traits characteristic of women and can work well in corporations today for the new global economy, instead of the overaggressive and overpowering styles of management in the past (Kanter, 1997).

A major obstacle to women to achieve managerial positions regards how they interact in the workplace. For example, being dependent, passive, unaggressive, noncompetitive, inner-oriented, empathic, sensitive, subjective, intuitive and supportive are traits typically associated with women, and are traits not considered appropriate for the demands of top management positions (Fagenson, 1990). Whether justified or not stereotypical attitudes regarding these traits considered feminine are prevalent in the corporate world, and women have to be prepared to deal with these concepts as they interact at the workplace. It is important to know that there are some barriers in the workplace, and also important to know that these barriers can be overcome (Fagenson, 1990).

Cultural socialization pressures push women toward the role of caretakers, rather than toward managerial careers, which reinforces gender role stereotyping. Other cultural factors that affect career plans for females include balancing career and family lack of role models, and lack of encouragement. Women in dual roles of job and marriage, express greater dissatisfaction about role overload more than married men. This is due to the belief that a man's career is considered more important than the wife's career (Cannings and Montmarquette, 2000).

In a study by Hagberg Consulting Group, in a survey that included 300 men and women, it was found that of the 47 management skills measured, women scored better than men in 38 skills. For example, the Hagberg study showed that women scored better than men in creating and articulating a vision, setting clear directions, being an inspirational role model, setting high standards for performance, and assuming responsibility (www.leadership-development.com, 2005). The Hagberg survey shows that women can be far better leaders than males, and questions why the glass ceiling holds women back.

The Hagberg study findings identify three reasons why women do not surpass the glass ceiling:

1. Women are reluctant about taking risk without covering all their bases, which causes them to not have opportunities to gain visibility that can lead to promotions in their organization.
2. Women are more group-oriented, which causes them to take on too much responsibility and tend to become more nurturing.
3. The way in which women present their ideas and plead for their cases, in that they do not simply present facts, but present facts in terms of right or wrong, make them appear defensive about their beliefs instead of assertive and confidence.

(www.leadership-development.com, 2005)

Some Women Still Play by the "Old Boys Club" Rules

Lavin (2004) cited conversations with individuals about how women's liberation is moving along and what women's liberation is actually accomplishing. A 50 year old woman stated that women are getting more management jobs, but when it comes to women's feelings and sense of worth there is some lacking. When women burned their bras in the 1960s, it was to be free and natural, though today many women, including professional woman, are still conforming to "sweater girl in a bullet-shaped bra" (Lavin, 2004, p. 2). As women have achieved professional success, many are playing upon their sexuality even more.

Lavin (2004) explains that women's liberation also liberated men, in that men no longer feel obligated to get married to have a sex life, and after being bachelors for 20 years being a husband is no longer appealing:

> What is the draw for a successful man to settle down with one woman when he can go through a series of them over the years? He has his home, his career, his toys and a regular supply of sex partners. (Lavin, 2004, p. 2)

Now, young women can burn their bras because they don't need them, yet, a large number of them increase their breast size, something that only movie stars did in the past. "We've come a long way, all right—all in the wrong direction" too often today (Lavin, 2004, p. 2).

Some women in the workplace also dress inappropriately, in a sexually suggestive way. In the last twenty years, dress codes in the workplace have been relaxed due to the changing nature of work and to foster employee satisfaction. However, women are still viewed very much on their appearance—clothes, hair and makeup are extremely important. It is essential for women to have a professional appearance in the workplace, but it is unprofessional for women to focus on their sexually physical attractiveness on the job (Bulletin to Management, 2001; HR Matters E-Tips, 2001).

Differences in Women and Men

There are distinctive differences in men and women in the way they interact with others and manage subordinates. In a study conducted in 1974, called the Bem Sex Role Inventory, it was identified that certain traits are widely associated with nurturing and expressiveness that are more feminine, while assertive, directive behavioral traits are more masculine (Howe, 1977). The Bem study supports the theory that men logically are more capable of leadership roles. Some extremist theories state that women are too emotional and erratic, fragile and moody to undertake leadership roles. Women perceive power as strength and energy, while men look upon power as having control. Men consider leadership to be top-down hierarchy with managers telling subordinates what to do, while women view leadership more collaboratively (Howe, 1977).

A statement by comedian, Elayne Boosler, is for humor, but it is true:

> When women are depressed, they eat or go shopping. Men invade
> another country. It's a whole different way of thinking. (Women in
> Management, 1999)

The workplace assumes that women are not cut throats and do not have the same "animal instincts" of men to compete in the business world (Smith, 2000).

Differences in Household Responsibilities by Gender

According to a report by the United Nations (1995), men and women utilize their time differently, and women work more hours per week than men do. However, much of women's work is unpaid domestic labor, i.e. housework and childcare, which to economists do not qualify as work. In most countries, women spend two times as many hours performing unpaid work than men do, and as much as nine times more in Japan. In industrialized nations women undertake two-thirds of domestic work. In the household, women tend to cook, do laundry, and clean the house, and iron, while men tend to do repairs and maintenance in the household. In most countries, women perform 75 to 90 percent of meal preparation and clean up. Additionally, women take on most of the childcare duties, particularly for young children. Consistently, in developing and industrialized nations, men perform childcare duties less than one hour each day, while women spend 5.2 to 10.7 hours per day solely on childcare. Women also perform most subsistence work for the household, such as gardening, and carrying water and wood in developing countries (United Nations, 1995). However, as times have changed regarding the role of women, increasingly men are taking on more roles caring for the children and elderly parents, particularly in industrialized countries (Clark, 1983).

In a report by the Associated Press (2005), the Japanese government Cabinet Office's Fiscal 2005 report states that Japanese women have difficulty in science fields when they are burdened by responsibilities at home with housework and child care; even though most homes have many modern electric appliances to lessen the household workload. This makes it difficult for Japanese women to continue their education after marriage, particularly in science fields. Japan has a lower percentage of women in science and technology fields than western countries. In 2004, "women made up 11.6 percent of Japanese scientific researchers, compared with 32.5 percent in the United States, 27.5 percent in France, and 26 percent in Britain" (Associated Press, 2005, p. 3A). Its post World War II constitution, written in 1986, requires the Japanese government to provide equality in workplace opportunities for women. A problem for Japanese women who have family responsibilities is that in Japan jobs require long working hours, which impedes working mothers from having careers and also hampers men from helping women perform domestic duties (Associated Press, 2005).

Walker and Best (1991) report that as women have moved in large numbers into the paid work force with careers in the last thirty years, this has reflected little change in husbands taking on more household work. However, women achieve psychological rewards from being employed. In the United States, women who work are happier and healthier, and have a lower rate of heart disease than homemakers or unemployed women (United Nations, 1995).

Education and Women

Until the twentieth century, women were barred from obtaining higher education in most countries. In the seventeenth century, education was limited for girls, and society taught girls that their education was insignificant. As late as the end of the nineteenth century, educator Edward Clarke stated that women's brains were relatively undeveloped and unsuitable to the rigorous demands of higher education. Additionally, Clarke argued that if women used too much of their energy to think, this could rob them of energy needed for their reproductive organs and they may become infertile (Koerner, 1999).

Today, philosophies espoused by men like Clarke are totally dismissed as women are obtaining access to higher education in large numbers and excelling in the workplace in all fields. In the U.S., it was projected that women will earn 57 percent of undergraduate degrees in 1999, compared to 43 percent in 1970, and 24 percent in 1950 (Koerner, 1999). However, in many countries, women obtain only 20 to 30 percent of undergraduate degrees, and in some countries even lower.

In institutions of higher education in the U.S., and in most countries, there is a shortage of women academic staff and senior management. Recent data shows that only 18 percent of full time professors are women. In 1975, only 46 percent of full time women faculty had tenure; and this statistic was still only 46 percent by 1992. In 1982, women full time professors earned 89 percent of what men earned as full time professors. In 1982, only 27 percent of all faculties were women, though women had earned 35 percent of Ph.D. degrees. By 1994, 31 percent of faculty was women, and women had earned 47 percent of all Ph.D. degrees (West, 1995). Page (2005) explains that while women are achieving significantly educationally, they are not closing the gender gap on income and power within the workplace. For example, women faculty at universities has dropped substantially in the last four years.

One problem regarding women and education is that female students tend to concentrate their studies in majors that are traditionally undertaken by females (Koerner, 1999). There are a low number of women in science and engineering studies in colleges. Additionally, technology still remains dominated by males. A small number of females enroll in advanced computer programming and graphics courses. Only 17 percent of computer science students are female. By 1996, women had obtained less than 28 percent of all undergraduate degrees in computer and information science (Fording, 1998).

Cisco Systems Corporation offers a 2-year course for high school students to certify graduates to become network administrators, and most students that enroll in this program are males (Koerner, 1999). Computer science and technology are high earning fields that are the wave of the future in this new global economy. However, women are only 25 percent of advanced technology in the workforce in the United States. In this new millennium, 65 percent of all jobs will require computer-related skills, and women must move toward these fields to meet the workplace needs of the coming years (Koerner, 1999).

The number of women in colleges of business has increased over the years; however, women are still underrepresented among graduates. In accounting, marketing, and other high profile, high paid fields in business, only 23 percent of graduates were women in 1998 (Koerner, 1999). Women are still reluctant to challenge the fields of math, computer sciences, and physical sciences as much as men. Women do not tend toward careers in physical sciences, agricultural sciences, engineering or business to have careers as scientists, businesspeople, and political leaders (Koerner, 1999). In the U.S., men that hold college degrees earn an average of $23,000 more annually than men who have high school diplomas, while women that have college degrees earn approximately $4,700 more annually than men who hold high school diplomas (Koerner, 1999).

Women and Poverty

Seventy percent of the world's poor are women. In the U.S., 60 percent of adults in poverty are women and more women than men head poor households. It must be noted that because women tend to outlive men and the elderly face more economic difficulties, this contributes to these statistics (Boo, 1996). According to recent studies, in industrialized nations three factors are important to women who live in poverty: strong family ties, job opportunities, and adequate social welfare (United Nations, 1995). These factors vary in different industrialized countries, particularly where the number of men and women in poverty are more equal. To assist women in poverty, there must be social and cultural support to help them juggle work and family responsibilities. It is important that they have jobs that pay sufficient incomes. Importantly, improved education opportunities and advancement in the workplace are essential to women lifting themselves from poverty (United Nations, 1995).

Gender Discrimination in the Workplace

A study conducted by Kilpatrick (1990), examines the job positions within a publishing company to ascertain the perceived nature of the job performed by gender. In the multiple-choice questionnaire for the Kilpatrick study, each answer was grouped in categories and 4 points were given for answers (See Table 3).

Table 3. Job Positions in Publishing Company by Gender

	Librarian Female Dominated	Truck Loader Male Dominated
Skill	570	430
Effort	580	590
Responsibility	470	390
Working Conditions	450	660
TOTAL	2,070	2,070

(Kilpatrick, 1990)

Table 3 shows that work performed by female librarians was rated quite equally to male truck loaders; while a librarian position requires a degree in higher education and a truck driver position is unskilled labor that requires little or no education. In the publishing company, the female librarians earned $3,000 less annually than the male truck loaders. As a result of the study, the pay of librarians was increased to be the same as truck loaders, but no more than the unskilled job (Kilpatrick, 1990).

Because women's jobs are perceived to require less competence, jobs considered "women's jobs" are stereotyped as being easier, requiring less intelligence, and valued less than jobs considered "men's jobs." Still today, "it is difficult for society to evaluate the value or worth of an occupation independent of gender labeling" (Kilpatrick, 1990, p. B).

Sexual Harassment

According to Fredrick and Atkinson (1997), gender roles are learned behavior in society. We are permeated daily with images of gender roles. For women the image is one of a sexual object, while men are presented as dominant individuals. As a result, when women are in the workplace gender images and roles can result in sexual harassment. Many men have not had to interact with women both professionally and personally, and while working with women they may result to a personal interaction, which can lead to sexual harassment.

It is difficult to know the extent of how often sexual harassment occurs in the workplace. Many women do not report sexual harassment incidents for various reasons, which include fear of losing their job, opting to leave their job, or somehow addressing the issue with the male co-worker to possibly stop the sexual harassment. Men can also experience sexual harassment, but most experts agree that women are most likely threatened with sexual harassment due to the female image of being a sexual object within society. Women in lower paying, lower status jobs are more likely to experience sexual harassment, which could be due to them appearing more vulnerable and desperate in their lower economic status as they work with dominate male supervisors on the job (Fredrick and Atkinson, 1997).

Some men are tempted to sexually harass a woman in a higher-level position to remind her of male power:

> An attempt is being made to undermine the woman's power or to diminish their accomplishments by reminding her of her vulnerably to sexual assault. Some feminist say this is indicative of the fact that many men resent women in positions of authority and so attempt to get the upper hand by asserting their sexual prowess. (Fredrick and Atkinson, 1997, p. 53.)

There are cases, when men look upon sexual harassment incidents as a romance or relationship with a woman co-worker, when the woman does not perceive it as romance (Fredrick and Atkinson, 1997). The U.S. government Employment Opportunity Commission defined sexual harassment:

> Unwelcome of sexual advances, requests for sexual favors, and other verbal or physical conduct of a sexual nature constitute sexual harassment when . . . submission to such conduct is made either explicitly or implicitly a term or condition of an individual's employment. (Fredrick and Atkinson, 1997, p. 55)

Coercive sexual harassment can be offering "something for something," *quid pro quo*, such as a promotion for a sexual favor. Uncoercive sexual harassment tends to be more verbal, such as sexual intimidation or annoyance, and is often considered less serious than coercive sexual harassment. (Fredrick and Atkinson, 1997).

Approximately a half of all women in the workplace in the U.K. will experience some form of sexual harassment during employment. Sexual harassment is negative and can definitely harm a woman psychologically. Today many young women are encouraged into non-traditional training, education and jobs for women where a high level of sexual harassment tends to occur (Bimrose, 2004). Rosener (1995) notes that in some organizations women employment is discouraged to avoid sexual harassment problems.

Smith (2000) explains that sexual harassment is highly misunderstood, and in the workplace some people avoid contact with the opposite sex to avoid a charge of sexual harassment; and are afraid that "You can't even tell someone they look nice without facing a sexual harassment lawsuit" (Smith, 2000, p. 125). Sexual harassment under federal guidelines has three major conditions: it must be on the basis of gender, unwelcome by the victim, and affects the term or condition of employment (Smith, 2000).

Concern with Low Salaries of Women in the Workplace

One reason that salaries for women are less than men is that historically, women have "crowded" into certain occupations. When women crowd a field, wages become depressed in the field. The reason that women crowded some fields in the past is possibly due to discrimination in more male-dominated fields; and the fact that women held less education than men before 1980, because women had less time due to child care and were not encouraged to seek better education (www.dol.gov, 2005).

In 1999, the six best paying fields held by women were: school teachers, secretaries, cashiers, managers and administrators, sales supervisors, and registered nurses. These six fields employed one-fourth of all women in the workforce. Of professionals, in 1995, the 4.4 million teachers consisted of 30 percent of women professionals. In 1995, women held 13 percent of management positions and had only 7 percent of executive positions (Fording, 1998; www.leadership-development.com, 2005).

According to Rosener (1995), various factors tilt the higher wage earnings for men:

1. Education and Experience Skills. Women do not have the educational skill levels and work experience to meet the same salary level as men to date.

2. Vocational Training. Women lag behind men in vocational trades gained through training and job tenure.
3. Job Choices with Trade Offs. Women tend to choose lower salary jobs as a trade off to get flexible hours, work at home, and part time work.
4. Job Commitment. Women's ties to family commitment can interfere with their careers and cause interruptions and delays in their careers that jeopardize their opportunities for promotions and advancement on the job.

(Fredrick ad Atkinson, 1997)

According to some theorists on women and work, women do not take the opportunities to take full time advantage of positions, which is the cause of wage discrepancy according to gender. However, other gender discriminatory factors come into play that causes women to receive lower salaries than men (Fredrick and Atkinson, 1997).

Changing Values in the Workplace

For the last twenty years, in corporate America values that are sometimes considered feminine values, such as being more detailed-oriented and working more closely with their work teams, have become acceptable in business. The new feminine corporate values are in conflict with traditional male-dominated corporate values of competition and authoritativeness. The feminine values are based on a new management approach regarding communication, leadership, negotiation, organizational structure, and control. The new feminine values are seen as the key to success for many businesses in the new global economy (Cameron, 1995).

As the twentieth century has ended, the workplace has changed to meet flexibility and innovations needed to meet the challenges of globalism and rapidly changing technology. Today, there is a shift to interactional norms and focus on flexibility, teamwork and collaborative problem solving, which are considered feminine oriented management traits (Cameron, 1995). Due to the fact that both feminine and masculine traits have value to organizations, it is important for organizations to create an organizational culture in which both styles of management are implemented and operate in synergy. The feminine traits of communication and teamwork are essential components to business success today (Kabacoff, 1998).

Leadership

Leadership is "the ability to teach, train, motivate, resolve conflicts, build an effective team and keep performance high" (Murdock, 1988, p. 25). Women have been leaders throughout history as homemakers, and today are leaders in management and executive positions in organizations and corporations. Effective leaders set goals and make plans to accomplish the goals. Leaders and managers are different. Leaders control the progress of each project, while not necessarily managing the project. Leaders delegate authority of subordinates and assess team members, but do not have to be the manager of the project. The effective leader is focused on accomplishment (Murdock, 1888; Lamsa and Sintonen, 2001).

In a study conducted by Sharpe (2000), leadership and personality were examined. There are four criteria for leadership styles in the Sharpe study:

1. Extraversion, which is more communicative.
2. Intraversion, in which a leader is distant from subordinates as they work.
3. Thinkers and feelers, in which leaders can gain information through senses or intuition; and use information as thinkers or feelers for decision making.
4. Judging and perceiving, in which leaders can organize by judging systematically or perceptively in a random or open-ended way.

(Sharpe, 2000).

Women tend to have leadership styles that are more intraversion, sensing and intuitive, as well as judging and perceiving. According to Sharpe (2000), women make effective leaders because they are able to make tough decisions while also being compassionate to others, and think through decisions better than men. Women outperform men in a variety of intellectual areas, which include producing high quality work, recognition of trends, and providing new ideas and acting on them. Women are better team builders, better listeners, understand mentoring better, and are more supportive than men (Bell, 2002).

Organizations Implement New Benefits

By the 1980s, because more women had entered the workforce, employers began providing more work-life benefits to compensate for the stresses of balancing work and family responsibilities (Clark, 1983). To deal with the large number of women now entering the workforce, organizations are increasingly striving to change cultural behaviors and attitudes within the organization. To better facilitate women on the job, time-based programs such as flexible hours and schedules, job sharing, and compressed workweek are being offered. Typically, flextime employees choose their own start and finish hours around a core period. Job sharing is when two part-time employees share one full-time position. Shorter or altered days, such as compressed workweeks, can also lessen the pressure for women in the workplace. All of these programs can help employees better juggle the conflicts of work and family (Markson, 1994).

Maternity leave and other attachment leaves have been introduced at many organizations to assist women employees with children. Attachment based programs can be pregnancy and childbirth leave, leave for early childcare or care of elderly parents, as well as parent day leave that can be used to care for an ill child or other family members. In 1993, in the U.S., the Family and Medical Leave Act was passed, which granted up to 12 weeks of unpaid leave from a job during any 12 month period to cope with family health problems, childbirth, adoption, and other family responsibilities. Male and female employees that take these leaves are guaranteed by law the right to return to their same position or an equivalent position. Though these new programs and laws are in place today to help employees with personal responsibilities, research shows that companies that have the best family oriented benefits have some of the worst records of promoting women, and this can be due to unwritten rules that punish employees who use these new personal-oriented benefits (Markson, 1994).

To help women, and some men who take on child care responsibilities and meet the demands of balancing work and home demands, employers are introducing new flex day programs in which employees can work four days per week, and have alternate times to start and end their work day. Employers are also allowing some employees to perform some of their work at home, which eliminates time traveling to and from work and gives employees time to undertake family duties throughout the day. Commuting to and from the job can be from two to four hours per day. Child care on the company premises is also being provided by some employers, as well as financial assistance to employees for child care and resources to employees for child care such as lists of child care providers (www.albany.edu, 2005). These employer initiatives are valuable to reducing employee stress at work and home. However, for certain types of jobs most flex time and other new personal benefits are not feasible. For example, a truck driver or medic can not change their schedules through flex time initiatives and must have other strategies to avoid stress like timing their days carefully so that they do not get overwhelmed with work and home roles.

New Organizational Models

Kolb, Williams and Frohlinger (2004) examine new phenomena in the business model of leadership, known as post-heroic. This model pertains to a move from command and control hierarchies where solutions were commanded from the top to a more integrated organizational structure that is collaborative through learning and which encompasses a more feminine style of leadership. It is perceived that this new model will facilitate the many women now in the workforce and help overcome new global challenges. This new model is a catalyst to employ more women in management, professional and executive positions. Business magazines today are quoting experts that explain "to boost business success with a great executive, hire a woman" (Kolb, Williams, and Frohlinger, 2004, p. 2). Women are cited with possessing eight qualities highly attractive to business success today: improv skills, relationship centric skills, less rank conscious, self-determination, trust, sensitivity, intuitiveness, and natural empowerment oriented toward intrinsic motivation (Kolb, Williams and Frohlinger, 2004, p. 2).

Overcoming the Obstacles

The road is still rocky for women in the workplace. Though 50 percent of management is women, only one percent is at top leadership in U.S. companies. Some CEOs state that the reason women have not advanced in corporate America to the highest positions of management is due to them not having been in management for very long. There is also an explanation that women have to opt out of their careers for marriage and family, which makes them less desirable for demanding top management and executive positions. Some believe that women are not competitive enough, and they hesitate to promote their accomplishments. It is also believed that women lack "presumption of credibility and competence when they take a leadership role" (Kolb, Williams and Frohlinger, 2004, p. 3).

Women are often tested when they take the lead of a company in four areas:

1. The Token Test, the belief that a woman has not actually earned her position at the top.
2. The Double Bind Test examines whether she can be a leader and a woman. This test looks at dominant traits, such as strength, decisiveness, aggressiveness and authoritativeness, which may seem overbearing for women, particularly if she is overly harsh, aggressive and uncaring.
3. The Fitness Test, questions whether she has the right qualifications and experience for the job, and cause women to be held to higher standards than men for a leadership position.
4. The Right Stuff Test, the belief that a woman must convince others that she has what it takes to be a leader.

(Kolb, Williams and Frohlinger, 2004)

Women should be aware that they would encounter these tests when they near or break through the glass ceiling. As women proceed at the top they must negotiate five challenges:

1. Intelligence and having significant information,
2. Backing key players to garner support,
3. Resources such as budgets,
4. Buy-in to bring momentum to their agenda, and
5. Making a difference in the organization.

(Kolb, Williams and Frohlinger, 2004).

To foster success for women in the workplace, organizations should value the qualities that make good leaders and develop leadership skills in both men and women managers. Training should be available to both men and women early in their careers. There should be opportunities for coaching, mentoring and networking. Women must be involved in all kinds of communication with the organization, formal and informal communication. All managers, men and women, should be involved in goal setting and decision-making. Women should have the same responsibilities and opportunities as men within an organization (Markson, 1994).

According to Morrison, White, Van Veslor, and the Center for Creative Leadership (1992), the glass ceiling still exists, and women are finding that younger men in corporations most frequently replace male executives over fifty. However, there are two new trends within corporate America that make placing women in management and executive level positions more attractive.

First, the country is becoming more diverse, and to respond to a more diverse market and customer base, senior executives are giving women and individuals of different races and ethnicity's more positions in higher-level management. Some examples of companies that have met the response of diversity are "Gannet, U.S. West, Avon, Corning, and American Express" (p. xii).

Another impetus that encourages companies to give women more executive positions is new legal and legislative pressures that were strengthened in the 1990s:

> The jury decision in 1991 to award a female supervisor of Texaco $20.3 million in damages for being unfairly passed over for promotion signals that sex discrimination within the management ranks can be detected by outsiders and punished (The Feminist Majority Foundation, 1991, p. 1).

Additionally, the federal government has taken action by ensuring that gender and race biases are removed from business practices in management within corporations (Morrison, Veslor, and the Center for Creative Leadership, 1992). In the Civil Rights Act of 1991, Congress passed a law for white women and people of color in hiring, promotion, as well as workplace relations; the Office of Federal Contract Compliance Programs (OFCCP) strictly enforces these guidelines. Additionally, the Glass Ceiling Commission study conducted by the Department of Labor in 1989, identified biases when there are "recruitment by networking, and lack of opportunities for people of color and women to take education programs and career-enhancing assignments" (Morrison, Veslor, and the Center for Creative Leadership, 1992, p. xiii).

To establish themselves in a male dominated work environment, women should have skills, courage and determination. Still today, men primarily conduct policymaking and job placement. Women must develop certain skills to survive in the male-dominated workplace. Women must plan a successful career path. Women tend to be less goal oriented about their career objectives than men. Women tend to look upon work as leading to personal growth and fulfillment. However, rising to the top requires hard work, dedication and long hours of work, which causes conflict for women who are balancing work and a family. To succeed in a professional career, a woman must focus on her career first for some period of her life, which is a great challenge when she has a family (Morris and Bennis, 1990).

Women must prepare themselves for competing. Competition is prevalent in the business world, and women must adopt the appropriate skills and behaviors needed to compete. Women must challenge perceptions of negative stereotypes of women leaders, which affect their promotion on the job. Typical stereotypical attitudes relative to women are that they are: soft, loving, attentive, intuitive, emotional, irritable, not objective, afraid of achievement, and cannot make tough decisions. All of these stereotypical assumptions may be false, yet these stereotypes influence the careers of women in management, their promotions and their future (Morris and Bennis, 1990).

Gaining recognition on the job requires doing good work. Yet, some women tend to contribute their success to luck instead of skill, which only fosters those negative stereotypes for women leaders. Some women with lack of self-confidence may have a fear of success, because they may perceive traits such as assertiveness and competitiveness as making them less physically attractive. Due to the stereotyping of women, some women put their initials on their resumes instead of their feminine full name (Morris and Bennis, 1990).

Women must continue growing and gain confidence. One of the most outstanding traits of successful people is that they keep on going in spite of the challenges and obstacles they face. Even when women successfully reach the door of success, others will keep them out if they are not assertive and persistent. To get ahead in the workplace, women managers must learn how decision makers think, and find ways to impress them, while avoiding compromising their morals and professional standards (Morris and Bennis, 1990).

To get ahead successful managers have to meet deadlines to foster the perception of performance. Women managers must learn to act or exercise their role as manager, and the power that is in the role of the manager. They must remember that their aim is to gain respect, and not love. Women managers have been characterized as supervising too closely, being overly concerned with details, fault finding, having an inability to delegate responsibility, and too emotional, which are traits that are signs of powerless people (Morris and Bennis, 1990).

Successful managers learn how to delegate to subordinates, and this is an area where many women have trouble. They must learn to analyze the job, decide what needs to be delegated, plan the delegation, select the person or persons to do the tasks, delegate, and follow up on delegated activities and tasks (Morris and Bennis, 1990).

Office Politics and Power

Women in management must become involved with office politics, which is where many women fail, because women tend to not like corporate politics and often do not understand the importance of it. They fail to comprehend the importance of informal systems within the organization and grasp the informal political system as a legitimate way to get things done. To succeed in an organization learning good political skills is essential. Being left out of the politics and "good old-boy" relationships within an organization can cause psychological impact, and outsiders may exhibit disengagement, resistance, lowered aspirations, and less determination to seek promotion and advancement (Morris and Bennis, 1990).

Power is strength, force and energy, and women must learn to understand power tactics. Having a mentor within the organization can be vital, because much essential information is passed down by word of mouth. Women must have someone within the organization that will recommend them and support them for promotions (Morris and Bennis, 1990).

Strategies to Succeed

There are a number of strategic techniques for approaching the challenges of the workplace for women managers. These techniques include: mentors, role models, networking to learn the business, developing coping strategies, focus, and effective style:

1. Mentors. A mentor can be someone higher in the organization with experience that can guide a protegee on how to get ahead in the organization. Mentors can help encourage, teach, and act as a sounding board to help protegees develop skills needed in their job. Mentors as sponsors can widen opportunities, help solve real problems, and serve as devil's advocate to provide challenges and give the protegee practice in asserting ideas and influencing others. As coaches, mentors can support protegees in finding what is important to them and what skills, interests and aspirations protegees have.

2. Role models. A role model can be anyone considered doing the right thing. By observing role models one can learn and adopt similar behaviors and actions. As someone seeks a role model, they should look for a person with characteristics they feel are needed to improve their life, someone that is outstanding. Adopting and adapting the

style of a role model can be an excellent way to learn flexibility in developing a professional style.

3. Networks. Networking is a process of gaining advice and moral support or using contacts for information to become more effective in the workplace. Women need other women to create a climate of support. Networks are valued for dealing with frustrations, sharing feelings about the job, and providing encouragement.

4. Developing coping strategies. To accomplish objectives in a male dominated culture, women must use sophisticated coping strategies in return. Women should make concessions in management style and skills, and cater to those preconceived stereotypes that can ultimately lead to the accomplishment of goals.

5. Focus. Focus on how you can advance in the company, and not on why you cannot.

6. Style. Women's leadership style tends to be transformational, which means getting workers to transform from self interest groups to broader, organizationally based groups. This style uses personal characteristics, such as charisma, personal contacts, and interpersonal skills, which are strong attributes of women. Women leaders in management are also more situations based, meaning they plan their strategies based on the situation at hand. On the other hand, men's leadership styles tend to be transactional. Men look upon their jobs as a series of transactions between them and their subordinates. Today organizations are requiring more participative management approaches, and women may have a natural style that enables them to move ahead easily in the new business environment.

(Stoner and Hartman, 1990).

According to Sherman (2001), in the workplace we face external or self-imposing obstacles that interfere with us moving forward, learning, growing, and succeeding in ways that are aligned with our own values and goals. To succeed in business, Sherman (2001) has identified ten power tools for advice and strategies:

1. Share your stories to help teach, inspire and motivate others. Be open and honest about telling other women what you have experienced to succeed and to fail. It is in the mistakes of your failures that others can better learn from your experiences.

2. Take charge of change by making it happen instead of letting it control your life and work.

3. Never stop learning, continue being inquisitive about more than your field.
4. Use crisis to gain wisdom. A crisis is not the end of the world, it is a personal test, for your personal life or work, and it is important to face challenge head on.
5. Become knowledgeable of technology, and stay abreast of innovations in technology.
6. Write out a life's mission to identify what you want to achieve and how you will achieve it. Have a mission plan for your personal life and business life.
7. Be a mentor to teach and be a role model to others. Mentor others and have a mentor for yourself.
8. Have a source of networking and nourish it. As you network think about how you can help others instead of just how others can help you. Networking is a two-way street.
9. Let your accomplishments be known as a way to wield power. Don't be afraid to brag about your achievements, and don't apologize for being powerful.
10. Give back. When you have achieved, help others achieve; it could be colleagues, charities, or any other that can benefit from what you have to offer.

(Sherman, 2001)

Williams (2004), attributes confidence of a woman, or man, as the key to what can garner success:

> I've met young women fresh out of the most prestigious schools in the country that just can't seem to get a break. And then I'll meet others who without finishing their degrees, have taken their career by the horns and have risen to the highest executive ranks. More than talent, more than skill, or than IQ, more than experience, your attitude is what gives you the edge. (Williams, 2004, p. 2)

Williams (2004) describes the attitude of success as "wildly sophisticated" in which you must be enterprising and creative to succeed. The attitude of success is take charge, don't let work define you, instead you define work; give your best, realize your potential and fulfil your dreams; challenge yourself, express yourself, push yourself to limits, and test your

The Pink Corner Office | 47

values and integrity. Let your work put a stamp on the world by having the attitude and strategies founded in success (Swiss, 2004).

In a study conducted by Swiss (2000), 52 men were queried to ascertain their perceptions of gender and power in the workplace. The study showed that men often gain confidence, comfort and power from being a male, though few think about their automatic male status. Men also suffer the same doubts and vulnerabilities in the workplace as women, but men tend to put on a bravado face about it, while women will openly show it and admit it (Swiss, 2000).

Gallagher (2000) points out strategies of wisdom that women executives and managers can use to be successful in their jobs. Importantly, don't win the battle, but lose the client. Sometimes an overachieving woman can work tremendously hard and get effective results in her tasks, but miss the big picture by assuring that her team at work and clients are not overstressed, pushed too hard, and alienated from her. Some CEOs complain of an overbearing, self-interest management style of certain women:

> Women focus too much on career advancement and not enough on their current responsibilities. When that happens, the corporation's interest can take a back seat. You can derail if you don't align the corporate interest with your self-interest (Gallagher, 2000, p. 41).

Gallagher (2000) describes four factors that determine success: competence, outcome, relationships and endurance. These four factors should work in conjunction and not be compartmentalized causing a manager to lose sight of the big picture. Gallagher (2000) identifies six lessons that shatter myths about success in business:

1. Focus on the big picture, because results are only a part of the story.
2. Create alliances throughout the corporation and the industry, but remember that networking is not necessarily a requirement for success.
3. Help others succeed, and avoid being ruthless to get to the top.
4. Be willing to take risks, don't be meek with your head down or you can get off the fast track.
5. Be yourself, because the man's game is not the only game around.

6. Find advocates, and don't just rely on one mentor; one mentor cannot pave the way for your success.

(Gallagher, 2000).

At all levels women are facing challenges in their efforts to advance within organizations:

> Further progress up the corporate ladder will require women to start taking risks, focusing their energy, and letting go of some details. Women should continue to communicate, develop, motivate staff, and lead by example. They need to stop getting mixed in the details, rescuing and mothering, and wearing their hearts on their sleeves. (www.leadership-development.com, 2005, p. 10)

Women Managers with Foreign Assignments

According to Adler and Izraeli (1994), while working as a manager in foreign countries, as an expatriate manager, typically a woman's effectiveness in a leadership role is influenced by how local women in the country succeed. However, in most cases, foreigners "see women expatriates as foreigners who happen to be women, not as women who happen to be foreigners" (Adler and Izraeli, 1994, p. 37). There is still uncertainty about sending women to work as managers in a foreign country due to cultural and traditional obstacles that may impede them from succeeding in international management.

CHAPTER IV

OUR FUTURE

The Future and Women in the Workplace

From 1998 to 2008, the workforce in the U.S. will rise from 140.5 million to 160.8 million, or 20.3 million additional jobs. This is a large number, which means that women have a big stake in the future regarding employment. From 1998 to 2008, it is projected that women in the workforce will increase 15 percent and men will increase 10 percent. It is projected that the fastest growing increase will be Hispanics and Asians, followed by blacks, then white women (Fording, 1998).

Much of the job growth in the next three years will be in teaching, computer positions, and health related fields. Executive, administrative and managerial positions will increase 16.4 percent by 2008; or 2.4 million more jobs, mostly in education, health care fields, finance, insurance and retail. Jobs that require an associates degree or higher-level degree in 1998 will increase to 40 percent in 2008 (Fording, 1998). At the end of the twentieth century, women, mostly in the fields of education and nursing, held 35 percent of professional positions. That number increased to 53.3 percent in 1999. Of the 20.9 million professionals, 11.2 million were women in 1999 (Adler and Izraeli, 1994).

Women are finding more opportunities in corporations due to the global economy:

> The best reason for believing that more women will be in charge before long is that in a ferociously competitive global economy, no company can afford to waste valuable brainpower simply because it's wearing a skirt. (Adler and Izraeli, 1994, p. 3)

According to McBroom (1986), many women of all economic levels are still influenced by personal histories and financial threads of the past. It must be noted that women today grew up with mothers of whom few had professional occupations, which deems male dominance still deeply rooted in our culture. Yet, considering traditional and historical influences, women in the workplace have achieved remarkable accomplishments in the last thirty years.

Women Are Now Empowered

Women have made significant strides in the workplace in the last thirty years as they moved into higher-level positions in large numbers. Women have continually moved up the ladder of success in corporate America in the brief period that many women have been in management and executive suites in the workplace. Women are now empowered:

> Women and girls are turning money, and education and resources into opportunity, freedom and power . . . reinventing the world. (Carr-Ruffino, 1997, p.7)

Eleanor Smeal, a former president of the National Organization for Women (NOW), describes a woman's place: "A woman's place is in the House, and the Senate, the executive suite, the boardroom" (Carr-Ruffino, 1997, p 41).

Findings

The analysis of published documents, and the original survey results associated with this book present a number of themes pertaining to the major issues regarding women in the workplace:

1. In the late twentieth century, in large numbers women successfully began breaking down barriers and moved into the workplace in non-management and management positions once deemed for men only.
2. There is a glass ceiling that prevents women in the workplace from advancing to the highest levels of management.
3. Women's salaries are less than men's salaries at all levels in the workplace.

4. Women still face discrimination in the workplace due to their gender.
5. Minority women face double discrimination in the workplace due to gender and ethnicity/race.
6. There is gender stereotyping that negatively perceives women to be less efficient than men in the workplace.
7. To succeed in higher level management and top executive positions women must cultivate strategies to beat men at "the man's game."
8. When women managers are assertive it is looked upon as being too overbearing, while men's assertiveness is considered appropriate and is seen as exercising power in the workplace.
9. Building successful careers in professional positions cause unique stresses for women in the workplace.
10. Women frequently face sexual harassment in the workplace.
11. Women are entering computer technology fields, the wave of the future, at a low rate.
12. In the past, a woman's historical and traditional role was relegated to being mother and wife in the household.
13. Boys and girls are socialized differently, and girlhood socialization focuses on preparing girls to become mothers and wives as adults.
14. Women are challenged in balancing workplace demands and household responsibilities.

CHAPTER V

OUR NEXT STEP

Summary

In 2000, women represented 40 percent of the workforce, and were 48.9 percent of management positions in the workplace (Gallagher, 2000). At all levels in the workplace and all fields, women now hold positions that only men held forty years ago. However, women face a number of challenges as they strive to succeed in the workplace. A major problem for women in management and professional positions is that they encounter a glass ceiling as they attempt to advance to top executive and senior management positions in organizations. The glass ceiling is in place in most organizations. It is an invisible barrier that blocks women from advancing to senior management and top executive positions. There is resistance from those at the top regarding women taking leadership roles at the highest echelons of organizations. In 1999, only 5.3 percent of women held top management jobs in Fortune 500 companies (Women in Management, 1999).

The glass ceiling and other obstacles to women at all levels of organizations are influenced by historical and traditional roles of women as mothers in the home and as sexual objects. Women are perceived stereotypically as inferior to men in society. Still today, many men look upon women as the weaker sex, and believe that a woman's place is in the home as wife and mother, her historical role (Ellig and Morin, 2001).

In the past, as children, boys and girls were socialized differently. Boys were given better education and encouragement to get a skill or become leaders when they become adults. While women were trained to do basic cooking and housekeeping duties to become wives and mothers as adults.

52

It was not expected that girls would grow up to become women with careers (Howe, 2005; Fredrick and Atkinson, 1997).

Before the nineteenth century, women were denied opportunities to enter most fields of work, and women executives or managers were primarily non-existent. Women's education was limited or non-existent before the nineteenth century, while it was expected that boys would gain an education. Few women gained higher education degrees, and those who did were expected to focus their lives on becoming a wife and mother, instead of fostering a professional career. In the nineteenth century, the only career open to women was schoolteacher (Howe, 1997; Fredrick and Atkinson, 1997).

In the early twentieth century many women obtained an adequate education, but few pursued careers or sought higher education; instead they still became housewives. Minority women faced a double standard against them, by gender and race. African American women have always worked to help support their families, but primarily in lower paying, lower status jobs until the civil rights movement of the 1960s and 1970s, when women and minorities demanded equal rights (Barnes, 2005).

Today, there is still a stereotypical perception that women are intellectually inferior to men, and that women are not proficient in leadership positions. There is a perception that women are not tough and smart enough. There is still gender discrimination in the workplace, and gender discrimination is difficult to detect, because it can be quite subtle (Smith, 2000).

Swiss (1996) state that in small and large companies there are differences in how women are treated and promoted. Women are less valued in the workplace than men are. The U.S. Department of Labor reported that in 1992, women's salaries were 72.2 percent of men's salaries, and that at all levels in the workplace women's salaries are less than what men earn. Women seldom receive bonuses for a job well done, while men typically receive bonuses for excelling at their job. Women's promotions are often overlooked, because there is a perception that women will get married and have children after a few years, and that her place in society remains in the home (Smith, 2000). A woman that excels is looked upon as an anomaly, and there is a widespread perception that women do not make effective leaders.

Initially, as women moved into the workplace in large numbers since the later twentieth century, to succeed they played the "man's game" by taking on more masculine, dominant approaches to their leadership styles. They modeled themselves after men by being aggressive and controlling. However, when women exhibited powerful, dominant attitudes in their leadership style, they were criticized for being overbearing and out of place; while these dominant, aggressive traits were considered attractive and expected for male leaders. At the same time, as women tried to take on dominant, assertive male attitudes and strategies to advance and lead in organizations, they were still expected to be feminine or they were considered inappropriate (Gearing, 2000). Thus, women in the workplace are faced with challenges as they strive to define themselves as leaders.

The challenges to succeed along beside men in the workplace can cause unique stresses to women. According to Gearing, as many as 87 percent of women in professional positions report that they experience unique stresses in the workplace. Women in management and executive positions must work 150 percent harder than men to succeed. Women professionals are left out of men's informal networking in organizations, such as golf courses and lounges at country clubs. Men as well as other women criticize women in leadership roles due to stereotypical perceptions of women as being incompetent (Gearing, 2000).

At all levels in the workplace, women are vulnerable to sexual harassment, and this includes women in management and executive positions. Many women do not report episodes of sexual harassment, yet it can be psychologically traumatic for a woman (Fredrick and Atkinson, 1997). In the U.K, it has been reported that as many as 50 percent of women have experienced incidents of sexual harassment (Bimrose, 2004).

By the 1990s, women began to learn how to better confront the challenges they face in the workplace. In the last ten years, women have started addressing and challenging issues that cause obstacles to their advancement by applying effective strategies and actions (Swiss, 1996). As women faced gender biases, they learned to strive for legitimacy by proving themselves capable of leadership positions. They learned how to dismiss stereotypical prejudices against a woman's capabilities. Importantly, women learned to succeed by utilizing their own style and found there was no need to play the "men's game" to succeed (Glaser and Smalley, 1995).

It has been identified that there is a difference between men and women, however, the differences does not make one gender more competent than the other. Men have certain strengths, while women overall have different strengths. Women tend to communicate and lead teamwork efforts more proficiently than men. Women began incorporating their feminine strengths into their leadership styles. Feminine leadership styles are characteristically more collaborative regarding working with staff, sharing tasks, and in win-win relationships for all employees, which women leaders undertake highly effectively (Glaser and Smalley, 1995). Women's style of management has become the new model for American corporations. It has been found that the feminine style of leadership is the most effective for success in the new global economy.

In some fields women do not yet have a large presence. Few women are in fields that involve engineering or science proficiency. This is due to the fact that fewer women major in fields at college requiring science or engineering, such as advanced computer information technology (IT) (Fording, 1998; Women in Wireless Communication, 2005).

Working in demanding jobs has presented another more personal challenge to women. Working women, particularly women in demanding professional careers, have to find ways to balance work versus family responsibilities. To focus on work, and household responsibilities such as rearing children and housekeeping, is at threat of being neglected. Giving priority to home and family can interfere with the focus women need to be successful in the workplace. While men have increased their household and childcare duties, many men do not take on a sufficient amount of family and household responsibilities to compensate for the wife working long hours or having demanding jobs (Gearing, 2000; Rosener, 1995; West 1995). Many women who work are still challenged with juggling work and family responsibilities.

Conclusion

This chapter finalizes this study on women in the workplace. In conclusion, women have succeeded in getting positions in the workplace in large numbers since the 1970s. However, to date, women in the workplace lack equal opportunities to men in a number of areas, regarding: promotions, standards of performance, pace of advancement, salaries, compensations, bonuses, opportunities to take professional risks, access to foster business relationships and networking, and support from top management. Even stellar performing women managers and executives face gender differentiation and exclusionary treatment.

The workplace still remains primarily a man's domain, particularly in higher-level positions in senior management and top executive positions. This is due to historical stereotypical perceptions of women, which are now being dismissed as women are proving their competence at all levels in the workplace. In the past, women were relegated to roles in the home rearing children, housekeeping, and being wives; now women can have fully enriched professional and personal lives. Before the mid-twentieth century, the best thing a woman could do in life was to marry a man who could support her; now a woman's happiness and well being in life are not determined necessar y by the man in her life. Today, she can choose to marry or not.

In the past, women were looked upon as intellectually inferior to men. Women's education was ignored or limited before the mid-twentieth century. Today, boys and girls are educated equally, and women now attend institutions of higher education in large numbers. Times have changed; however, women still hold the major responsibility for rearing children and household duties, their traditional role, along with their job responsibilities. However, parenting is the most difficult responsibility that human beings undertake. Like the certainty of paying taxes and death, parenting always presents one's greatest challenge regardless of social changes or changes in family dynamics. Therefore, difficulties are encountered for women who manage dual roles.

The important point regarding this entire topic of women in the workplace is that women have changed their role in society and are now empowered significantly. That is a tremendous accomplishment, which is phenomenal in terms of social change, because social change typically manifests slowly, historically. Women are no longer destined to become only housewives and mothers. Women are now excelling in jobs and careers, at all levels and in all fields.

Today, all industrialized countries are including women in the workplace for management and executive positions. Today, women from all economic levels and ethnicities can evolve and make great professional achievements that give them economic freedom, which was unimaginable fifty years ago. In Germany, Chile, and Ghana, women were elected president in 2006. The Ghanaian president is the first woman elected president in an African nation. In the U.S., for the first time there is serious discussion about a woman having the chance to be elected president. Historical perceptions regarding women being inferior to men only linger, and, today, weakness and inferiority are not the general perception of women. Women have indeed made great progress advancing in the workplace; thus, their personal lives and all of society are transformed for the betterment of mankind. It is important to note that women have been in the workplace in large numbers and holding many leadership positions in organizations for only the last thirty years. Yet, they have advanced tremendously, and the future holds great promise.

Recommendations for the Next Step

A number of recommendations can be proposed in response to this book. The greatest problem within the workplace regarding women's advancement pertains to the strategies that they must implement to promote professional growth and advancement. How women facilitate strategic management styles pose the greatest challenges to women in the workplace; and effective style of management negates undue stereotypical perceptions of women.

Women's organizations can be highly instrumental in promoting women's advancement in the workplace. Women foster women's organizations to help other women succeed in the workplace. Women who do succeed should make themselves available to assisting other women moving up the ladder of success in organizations through initiatives that include mentoring, networking, role modeling and professional support. Professional women need to make themselves more available to help guide other women to success in the workplace. Women's organizations can be essential to providing information on professionalism and success strategies for women in the workplace at all levels, including senior management and top executive positions. Through women's organizations, successful women can assist other women in all fields. Women's organizations can also provide resources and information on how to avoid or alleviate the unique stresses that women may face as they strive to succeed in the workplace. Additionally, women's organizations can work to encourage education policymakers to urge girls in high school and junior high school to become interested in math and science studies, which would be essential to women having a larger presence in fields that require engineering and science proficiency.

Another recommendation that women can consider is going into business by starting their own companies. Many men that excel in a field or industry start their own company. Women should become more daring and also consider going into business when they know a skill or their field well. This way, women will own more companies, and women will have increased power in decisions regarding who gets top positions.

Women should also use their buying power, which is $3 trillion annually, to urge corporations to more actively finance programs in women studies departments in universities. Women's studies departments should have far more courses that debate the many issues pertaining to women in the workplace, and financing for these programs should be supplemented by corporations.

After 30 years, it is unfortunate that research is inadequate in the area of women in the workplace. Women studies departments are arising in a number of universities across the country and the topic of women in the workplace should become a focal point for research in order to gather more information on the topic.

Figure 1: Survey Question No. 1 Results

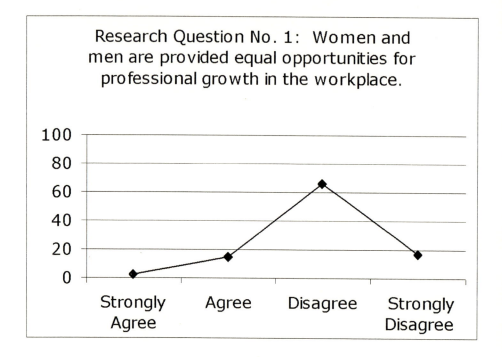

Figure 2: Survey Question No. 2 Results

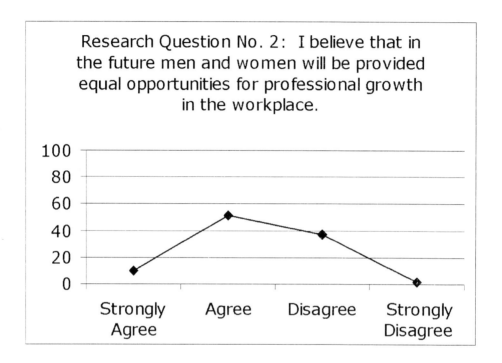

Figure 3: Survey Question No. 3 Results

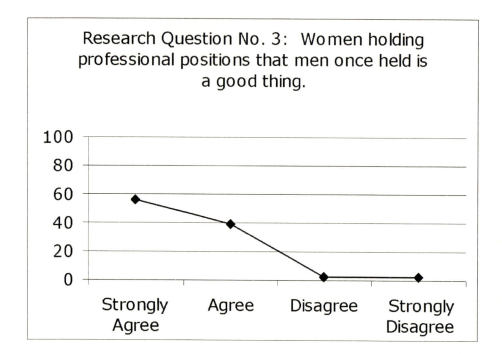

Figure 4: Survey Question No. 4 Results

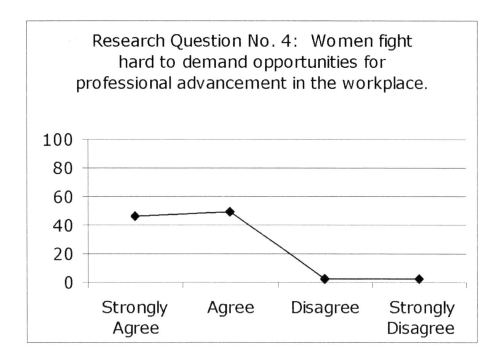

Figure 5: Survey Question No. 5 Results

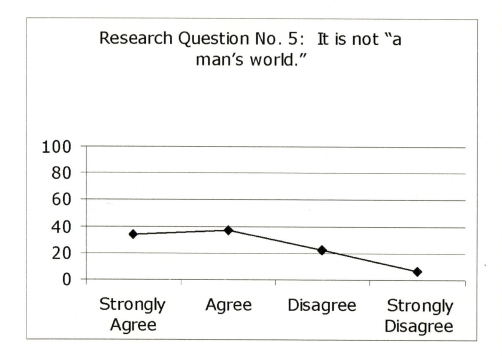

Figure 6: Survey Question No. 6 Results

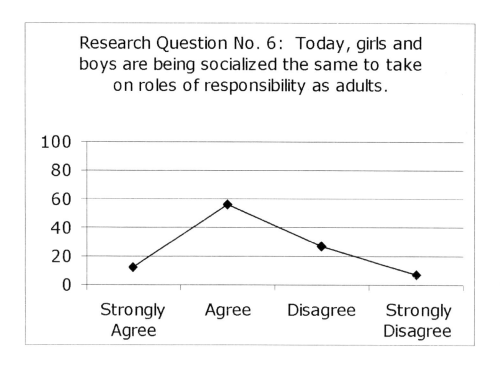

Figure 7: Survey Question No. 7 Results

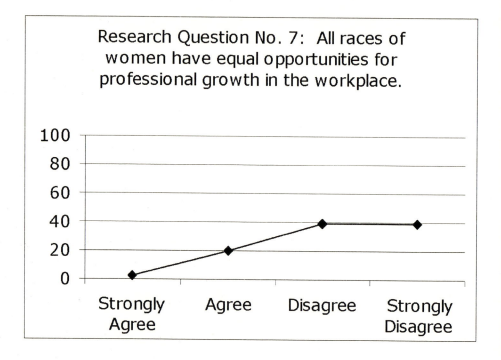

Figure 8: Survey Question No. 8 Results

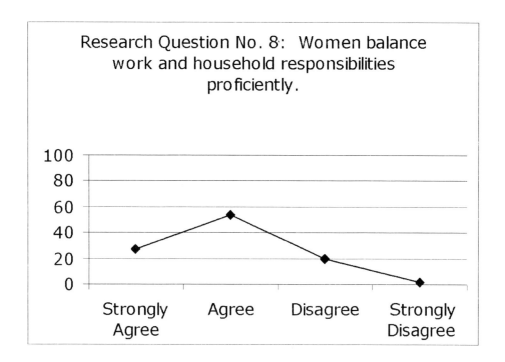

Figure 9: Survey Question No. 9 Results

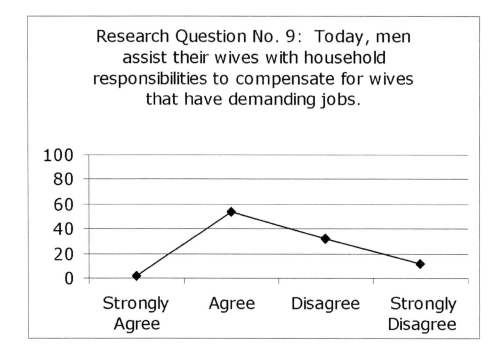

Figure 10: Survey Question No. 10 Results

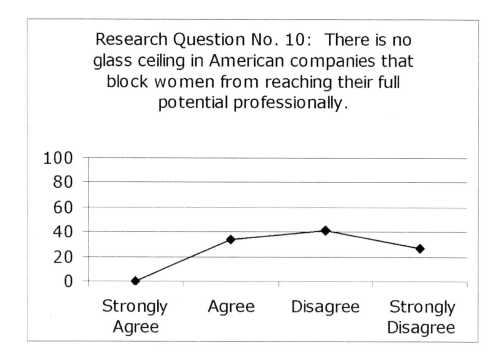

INDEX

List of Tables

Table 1. Ratio of Women to Men in Administrative Positions 21

Table 2. Glass Ceiling Perks are Different for Men and Women 22

Table 3 Job Positions in a Publishing Company by Gender 34

List of Figures

Figure 1: Survey Question No. 1 Results. 58

Figure 2: Survey Question No. 2 Results. 59

Figure 3: Survey Question No. 3 Results. 60

Figure 4: Survey Question No. 4 Results. 61

Figure 5: Survey Question No. 5 Results. 62

Figure 6: Survey Question No. 6 Results. 63

Figure 7: Survey Question No. 7 Results. 64

Figure 8: Survey Question No. 8 Results. 65

Figure 9: Survey Question No. 9 Results. 66

Figure 10: Survey Question No. 10 Results. 67

REFERENCES

Adler, Nancy J., and Izraeli, Dafna (1994). *Competitive frontiers: Women managers in a global economy.* Cambridge, Massachusetts: Blackwell Business.

Affirmative Action (2005). www.affirmativeaction.org.

Alasuutari, Pertti. (1998). *An Invitation to Social Research.* London: Sage Publishers.

Albany University. (2005). www.albany.edu.

Alfred, Mary. (2005). Does Wisconsin women work? Perceptions of participating women and their employers. *Journal of Family and Economic, Issue* 26, No. 3, pp. 345-370.

Ash, Mary Kay. (1981). *Mary Kay.* New York: Harper & Row.

Associated Press. (2005). Workplace support sought in Japan: Women struggle with chores, kids. Chicago, Tribune, June 15, 2005, p. 3A.

Austin, Linda. (2000). *What's Holding You Back.* New York: Basic Books.

Barber, Elizabeth Wayland. (1994). *Women's work the first 20,000 years.* New York: W.W. Norton & Co.

Barnes, Sandras. (2005). *Connecting theory to professional growth and pedagogical practices in a multicultural setting.* Lesley College. www.Lesley.edu/journal/ppp/2barnes.html

Bimrose, Jenny. (2004). Sexual harassment in the workplace: An ethical dilemma for career guidance practice? *British Journal of Guidance and Counseling*, Vol. 32, No. 1., February 2004, p. 109-121.

Black Collegian. (2005). www.black-collegian.com

Boo, K. (1996). Two women, two responses to change. *Washington Post*, December 15, 1996, pp. A1, A28-A29.

Brown, Clair, and Peachman, Joseph A. (1987). Gender in the workplace. Washington, D.C.: The Brooking Institute.

Brown, Jordan. (1989). *Elizabeth Blackwell*. New York: Chelsea House.

Bulletin to Management, Women's Appearance Affects Job Prospects, Workplace Advancement. (2004). *Bureau of National Affairs, Inc.*, Washington, D.C., Vol. 52, No. 25, 6/01.

Bundles, A'Lelia. (2001). On her own ground: The life and times of Madam C. J. Walker. New York: Scribner.

Cameron, Deborah. (1995). Verbal Hygiene. www.verbalhygiene.com.

Cannings, Kathleen, and Montmarquette, Kathleen. (2000). Managerial momentum: A simultaneous model of the career progression of male and female managers. *Industrial and Labor Relations Review*, Vol. 44, pp. 212-228.

Carr-Ruffino, Norma. (1997). The promotable woman: 10 essential skills for the new millennium. Third Edition. Franklin Lakes, NJ: Career Press.

Catalyst. (2000). Equal pay and highest executive ranks still elude women. www.catalystwomen.org.press

Caudron, S. (1994). The concrete ceiling. *Industry Week*, July 4, 1994, p. 31-36.

Cava, Roberta. (1988). *Escaping the pink collar ghetto: How women can advance in business*. Ontario, Canada: Key Porter Books.

Center for Women in Business Research. (2002). African American women owned businesses in the United States, 2002: A fact sheet. www.womensbusinessresearch.org.

Cicourel, Aaron V. (1964). *Method and Measurement in Sociology*. New York: Free.

Clark, Dorothy Wilson. (1983). *I will be a doctor!* Nashville, TN: Abingdon Press.

Davies, Richard E. (1984). *Handbook for Doctor of Ministry Projects: An approach to structured observation of ministry*. Lanham, MD: UP of America, 1984.

Drucker, Peter. (1994). The age of social transformation. *The Atlantic Monthly*, Vol. 274, p. 53-80.

Eisler, Raine. (1997). The hidden sub-text for sustainable change: The new business of business. *Sharing responsibility for a positive global future*. www.globalfuture.com

Ellig, Janice Reals, and Morin, William J. (2001). *What every successful woman knows: 12 breakthrough strategies to get the power and ignite your career*. New York: McGraw-Hill.

Fagenson, Ellen (1990). At the heart of women in management research: Theoretical and methodological approaches and their biases. *Journal of Business Ethos*, April/May 1990, pp. 267-274.

Feminist Majority Foundation. (1991). Empowering Women in Business. Washington, D.C., Feminist Majority Foundation, pp. 1-5).

Fording, L. (1998). Computing club: Boys only? *www.newsweek.com*, October, 14, 1998.

Fowler, Floyd J. (1984). *Survey Research Methods*. Beverly Hills: Sage Publishers, 1984.

Fredrick, Candice, and Atkinson, Camille. (1997). *Women, Ethics And The Workplace*. New York: Praeger.

Gall, Meredith D., Gall, Joyce P., Borg, Walter R. (2003*). Educational research: An introduction*. New York: Allyn and Bacon.

Gallagher, Carol, and Golant, Susan K. (2000). *Going to the top: A road map for success from America's leading women executives*. New York: Viking.

Gearing, Sylvia. (2000). Female executive stress syndrome: The working woman's guide to a balanced and successful life. *The Summit Group*, pp. 27-47.

Glaser, Connie, and Smalley, Barbara Steinberg. (1995). *Swim with the dolphins: How women can succeed in corporate American on their own terms*. New York: Warner Books.

Glazer, Penina Migdal, and Slater Miriam. (1987). *Unequal colleagues: The entrance of women into the professions, 1890-1940*. New Brunswick: Rutgers University Press.

Grant, J. (1988). Women as managers: What they can offer to organizations. *Organizational Dynamics*, Vol. 16, pp. 56-63.

Hirsh, Wendy, and Jackson, Charles. (1989). Women into Management: Issues influencing the entry of women into management jobs. www. womeninmanagement.com.

Howe, Louise Kapp. (1977). *Pink-collar workers: Inside the World of Women*. New York: Putnam.

HR Matters E-Tips. (2001). Dress Codes That Differentiate Between Men and Women: Personnel Policy Service Inc. http://www.ppspublishers. com/hrmtips.htm

Investing for Women. (2001). http:/womensinvest.about.com/money/womensinvest/blmarykay.htm, July 3, 2001.

James, Angela. (1999). *Black women in the labor force.* Department of Sociology. University of Southern California.

Kabacoff, Robert. (1998). Gender differences in organizational leadership: A large sample study presented at the Annual American Psychological Association, 1998.

Kamil, Michael L. (2004). The current state of quantitative research. *Reading Research Quarterly,* January-March, 2004, 39(1), 100-107.

Kanter, Rosabeth Moss. (1997). On the Frontiers of Management. www.frontiersofmanagement.com.

Katz, Montana. (1996). *The gender bias prevention book: Helping girls and women to have satisfying lives and careers.* Northvale, New Jersey: Jason Aronson, Inc.

Kilpatrick, L. (1990). In Ontario: Equal pay for equal work becomes a reality, but *not very easily. The Wall Street Journal,* March 9, 1990, p. B.

Koerner, B. I. (1999). Where the boys aren't. *U.S. News and World Report,* February 8, 1999, pp. 46-50, 53-55.

Kolb, Deborah M., Williams, Judith, and Frohlinger, Carol. (2004). *Her place at the table: A woman's guide to negotiating five key challenges to leadership success.* San Francisco, CA: Jossey-Bass.

Kuzel, Anton J. (1999). *Sampling in qualitative inquiry: Doing qualitative research.* 2nd ed. Eds. Benjamin F. Crabtree and Williams L. Miller. Thousand Oaks, CA: Sage Publishers.

Lavin, Cheryl. (2004). Tales From The Front. *Chicago Tribune,* July 21, 2004, p. 2.

Leadership Development. (2005). www.leadership-development.com

Leathwood, Carole. (2005). Treat me as a human being, don't look at me as a woman: Femininities and professional identities in further education. *Gender and Education*, Vol. 17, NO. 4, October, 2005, pp. 387-409.

Lepage-Lees, Pamela. (1998). Education and women's resiliency Exploring the experiences of successful women from the disadvantaged backgrounds. *Advancing Women in Leadership Journal*, 1998.

Let's Talk Business Network. (2001). www.ltbn.com

Life Application Bible. (1989). *Genesis 2: 18-23 and proverbs 31: 10-31*. Wheaton, IL: Tyndale House Publishers, Inc.

Lougheed, Jacqueline. (2000). Attitudes toward women leaders analyzed by gender and occupation. *Advancing Women in Leadership Journal*, 2000.

Mankiller, Wilma, and Wallis, Michael. (1993). *Mankiller a chief and her people*. New York: St. Martin's Press.

Markson, Elizabeth. (1994). Will men ever accept the woman manager? *Industry Week*, July 4, 1994, pp. 31-36.

McBroom, Patricia A. (1986). *The third sex: The new professional woman*. New York: William Morrow and Company, Inc.

Morris, Michele, and Bennis, Warren. (1990). Taking charge in a different way. *Working Women*, Vol. 9, March 1990, pp. 73-79.

Morrison, Ann M., White, Randall, Van Veslor, Ellen, and the Center for Creative Leadership. (1982). *Breaking the glass ceiling: Can women reach the top of America's largest corporations?* Reading, Massachusetts: Addison-Wesley Publishing Company.

Naiman, Sandy. (1999). Debbi Fields is one smart cookie. *Toronto Star*, 18 Jan 1999.

Odell, John. (1998). *Qualitative Research Design*. Los Angeles: University of Southern California. www.rcf.usc.edu/-odell

Page, Clarence. (2005). Men losing their pedestal status. *Chicago Tribune*, January 26, 2005, p. 19.

People Management. (1998). Vol. 4, No. 22, November 1, 1998, p. 21.

Rosener, Judy B. (1995). *America's competitive secret: Women managers*. New York; Oxford University Press.

Sharpe, Pamela. (1996). *Adapting to capitalism: Working women in the English economy*. New York: St. Martin's Press Inc.

Sherman, Aliza. (2001). *Powertools for women in business: 10 ways to succeed in life and work*. New York: Entrepreneur Press.

Shields, Cydney, and Shields, Leslie C. (1993). *Work sister work*. New York: Carol Publishing Group.

Silver, David A. (1994). *Enterprising women: Lessons from 100 of the greatest entrepreneurs of our day*. New York: Amacom, American Management Association.

Small Business, 2002. (2002). Wells Fargo publisher.

Smith, Dayle M. (2000). *Women at work: Leadership for the next century*. Saddle River, NJ: Prentice-Hall, Inc.

Stoner, Charles, and Hartman, Richard. (1990). Family responsibilities and career progress: The good, the bad, and ugly. *Business Horizons*, May/June 1990, Vol. 33, p. 7-14.

Swiss, Deborah. (2000). *The male mind at work: A woman's guide to working with men*. Cambridge, Massachusetts: Perseus Publishing.

Swiss, Deborah. (1996). *Women breaking through: Overcoming the final 10 obstacles at work*. Princeton, New Jersey: Peterson's/Pacesetter Books.

Swoboda, F. (1995). Law, Education Failing To Break The Glass Ceiling. *Washington Post*, November 25, 1995, pp. C1-C2.

Tetreault, Mary Kay Thompson. (1978). *Women in America: Half of history.* New York: Rand McNally & Co.

United Nations. (1995). The world's women 1995: Trends and statistics. New York, United Nations.

Walker, L. O. (1991). Well Being Of Mothers And Infant Children. A preliminary comparison of employed women and homemakers. *Women and Health,* 17(1), pp. 71-89.

West, M. S. (1995). Women faculty: Frozen in time. *Academe,* 81(4), 26-29.

Williams, Nicole. (2004). *Wildly sophisticated: A bold new attitude for career success.* New York: Perigee Book.

Women In Management. (1999). *Women leaders in corporate Canada: Twelve women head Financial Post 500 companies.* London Ontario: The University of Western Ontario.

Wright, John W. (1996). *The American Almanac Of Jobs And Salaries.* New York: Avon Books.

U.S. Department Of Labor. (2005). 2005 Report. www.dol.gov/dol/wb/public/wb_pubs/wagegap2000.htm

U.S. Department of Labor. (2000). Women's Earnings A Percent of Men's, 1979-2000.

UWYO. (2005). www.uwyo.edu.

BVG